CAPE POETRY PAPERBACKS

TED WALKER

BURNING THE IVY

by the same author

FOX ON A BARN DOOR
THE SOLITARIES
THE NIGHT BATHERS
GLOVES TO THE HANGMAN

Ted Walker

BURNING THE IVY

POEMS 1973–77

JONATHAN CAPE
THIRTY BEDFORD SQUARE LONDON

First published 1978

Jonathan Cape Ltd
30 Bedford Square, London WC1

British Library Cataloguing in Publication Data
Walker, Ted
Burning the ivy.
I. Title
821'.9'14 PR6073.A4B/
ISBN 0-224-01637-7

ACKNOWLEDGMENTS

The poems 'Night rain' (1971), 'Vipers' (1974), 'Stanzas for the graves' (1975) 'Moving' (1977) and 'Mountain ponies' appeared originally in the *New Yorker* and were copyrighted © in the respective years shown by The New Yorker Magazine, Inc. Thanks are also due to: the South-East Arts Association, the Arts Council of Great Britain, the Globe Playhouse Trust, the Southern Arts Association, the Borestone Mountain Poetry Awards 1975, P.E.N., the Poetry Book Society, the *Boston University Journal*, the *New Statesman* and the *Observer*.

Printed in Great Britain by
The Anchor Press Ltd, and bound by
Wm Brendon & Son Ltd, both of
Tiptree, Essex

Contents

FOR MARGARET

Moving

Do not attempt to sleep – your strangeness
Arouses the new house. Amazed floors,
Unaccustomed yet to what is yours,
Shift to the burden of what you bring;
Overhead, the loft that encloses

A fresh store of sentimental junk
Creaks from your broken bits of childhood.
Sometimes maybe it's all to the good
To touch, to rearrange all you own
Elsewhere. But in someone else's sink,

Though it's yours now and paid for, even
A cup can remind you of who you are,
And what you were, and why you are here.
From choice, or by accident, or both,
Once more you've humped your stuff. The oven

Was worst, its squat, impervious bulk
Grudging each inch. Yet plain heaviness,
Lifted and lifted, doesn't oppress
Like those gross abstracts we can't dispose
Of. They arrive with the morning milk.

Christmas apples

Year-long, weekdays, I pass an orchard.
Mornings, where its windbreak poplars are,
The engine warms and I change into top
Toward the day. There's nothing to see
Of fruit-trees from the road. Blossom-time,

A dry thaw of blown petals may sift
To the ditch, soon gone; and winter nights,
When I slow for the corner near home,
Sometimes I picture the stiff ballet
Of trees imploring frost from starlight:

But, back in the warmth, forget them. Once
A year – a Sunday in December –
I drive to a warehouse at the heart
Of an acreage seeming vaster than
Memory tends. Black banners, crows flutter

High over the fields. I park the car
In an empty lot, walk to the edge
Of the same, leafless plantation where,
A twelvemonth since, my face to the wind,
I laid by the sorrows of a year.

There's been another death: though by now
It has sunk under, like the water
Of small snow that fell the day I heard.
Once again (though to remember them
Is an ice along the skull) I call

To mind the gradually dying
Who haunt, more accusing than the dead,

These days I riffle at another
Year's end. Month by month I have screened
Their lives from mine; today each mindful hurt

That love inflicts in fostering love,
Each mindless act of chronic neglect
That dismembers a friendship alive,
I would undo. In exact patterns,
Yet frantic as drowners, apple-trees

Lift bare arms into the shortest day.
I'll not see them bud, burst into leaf,
Bloom, or their limbs bend when summer dust
Falls: my road leads by and beyond them.
Behind me somebody slides the door

And I turn and stare blank in a blank
Hangar. An appalling fragrance spills.
I breathe apples in before I see them,
Laxtons and Coxs, rack upon rack,
Shocking as a wiped-out flock of birds.

Ivy

Nine years ago I killed the ivy:
But once more it swarms the ancient wall
Round my plot. It has grown top-heavy
And rank, too much for the bricks to bear;
Powdery mortar has begun to fall

As fall it did our first winter here,
Eaten away by ravaging roots.
Ripened, the poison berries cluster;
Black swags in the February wind
Loom over my soil. A sleet shower starts

As I place the ladder, climb high and
Straddle the coping. Evergreen leaves
Conceal dust of dead seasons. I find
The wren's nest we hunted for one spring;
A ball; a lost doll that falls in halves

In my hands. Engrossed now, clambering
On, I incise with new secateurs
The tangle of years. Dismembering
Thick, reptilian stems, my palm bleeds;
I grasp sticky lushness. For the hours

It takes to shear clean my fifty yards
Of masonry, all is forgotten
Of what gnaws my present self. Last birds –
Rooks and lapwings – fly above a house
That once was not mine, will not be mine

One day; unfamiliar, those windows
Lit one by one and uncurtained yet
Against the dark. Another nine years,

Another, someone must grub up trunks
As I tomorrow shall in the wet

Field outside the wall. A blunted axe
He'll bring back, whoever he may be.
As long as I hone its edge, I'll give thanks
For the task. Duly, as men have done
Their several times each century

Since the bricks were laid, one morning soon
I'll re-point the gaps creepers have picked
Between them. I'll watch my ivy burn,
Tendrils of flame clinging to the flat
Surfaces of night; will sense what hacked

Vines will grip again, cannot be kept out.

Stanzas for the graves

Rain had eased, an end-of-summer rain
Over Wales. Soon the sheened chapel roof,
Its wet slate tinctured like a rubbed plum,
Would dull, drying back into its bloom.
Day's lustre drained as late afternoon

Entered evening. Bringing autumn flowers,
Jagged dahlias, we trod coarse gravel
Away from laughter – stubbed cigarettes
And jokes while my friend spent his minutes
With dead kin, people I never knew.

The way was hard from the iron gate.
Marauding bracken and ripe blackberries
Stifled paths among forgotten graves
And graves half-forgotten, where black leaves
Rotted in sundry vessels chosen

With special care not so long ago.
I was a total stranger. No one
Lay in this ground to whom I might owe
My tepid, my true, my trumped-up awe,
Respect, remorse, or plain, wholesome love;

A neutral I came, shy guest without
Acquaintance at a party. I stood
Apart against an awkward headstone.
With nowhere to sit, to be alone,
I stared out over the pocked valley

Where nobody at that moment chose
To hang out washing, wheel a barrow
Of tools from a garden shed. I said
I'd fetch water. And as I half slid,
Half fell, scrambling down amid the crush

And clamour of these who wore their names
Like delegates at a convention,
I learned their ages, knew who loved whom
For how long and how much. Not for them
Had I felt pain of loss; but neither

Could I accord them that indifference
With which so casually I snub
Unimpinging billions of the quick.
I turned the tap on full, rubbed the muck
From a glass jar, filled it to the brim.

For all those who cannot be disowned,
Whose lives have not been marked with costly
Marble, I remember, with this, how
Strident were the flowers as the dusk grew
Around us. But not for them alone

I make my elegy. Imminent
Dead, you whom I love negligently,
Often hurt, and sometimes disremember,
Know how, as we left for the umber
Dark, I saw all your eyes, alive as stars.

Elegy for an old acquaintance

Give sorrow words: the grief that does not speak
Whispers the o'erfraught heart, and bids it break.
(*Macbeth*, IV, iii)

Before true autumn the sun
  has less than warmth of flesh
and the days fall golden-green
  as the smooth rind of quinces;
to face into such sunlight
  is like bathing in milk.

And yet we have no name for
  the year's blandest interim
before the breath turns rancid
  in the mouth of October,
while the hours pour languidly
  upon themselves like oils.

Nor, as I hear you are dead,
  sometime, casual friend, have I
words for what is less than grief
  but more than common sorrow.
All our lives we prepare
  for the vaster bereavements:

every day, in case they die,
  I kill my children in my mind.
But no time is apt for the death
  of those we owe almost love –
a liking beyond affection;
  of those we seldom visit

but are always glad to see.
  Our stored tears are not for them
whose lives are but particles,
  not masonry of our own.

Their elegies are for ourselves,
   our parings, our bits of dead
skin. It is a nameless season
   of small mourning the heart keeps

every day that comes. I would wish
   to name its tart fruits of regret:
whatever it is we feel, making
   acknowledgment of minor loss,
of meagre failure, of yielding
   to time what was ours for good;

what shall we call those calendars
   of all unmemorable decay?
Old friend, if I speak no grief,
   yet know I am not untouched
by what you do so untimely.
   They are yours, the small, final

roses opening scentless in my garden.
   I spend an empty afternoon
watching the summer's end; this air
   I breathe from the quenched stubble-
fires fusts on the lung. It is for all
   us living, inarticulate, small

sorrowers my heart lurches now
   as I gag towards the sun;
for us all notice the lichen
   on the wall bounding what is mine
and sense what feeble, savage-rooted growths
   pick at the fabric of happiness.

Night rain

I hear rain begin. It is rain
has brought me out of sleep. I hear
from a dream stiff ashes of paper

uncrinkling on brick. It is rain
stopping upon heavy roses
holding me from tomorrow;

it is the rain's moments I borrow
for this listening. Yet it loses
me to the sun, and I am back

among yesterday's warm shadows
under the pergola. There glows
along my grateful skin a week

of opening blooms. I have brought
into my garden everyone
I love, even those an ocean

separates, to share the taut
perfection of the unscented bud
and the waxen feel of the leaf.

I wish them all roses – though if
it were in my gift, surely I'd
keep back the sound of rain on them

by night. Trying not to disturb
the settled house, I let a blob
of collecting water fall on a stem

under the window I ease. Scents
rise and enter from the wet flowers
I cannot see. Were I to close

them out, there would be left the sense
of them in an empty dark to keep
me vigilant. Though I were not here

they would breathe in this room. I suffer
the rain sometime to offer me sleep.

For his old English master
(Paul Coltman, on his retirement)

Wrought-out winter's prolonged avarice over, now
Plush June's red is a firm bargain of swollen buds;
Frost-hung meadows of fieldfares are a memory
Now one swallow suggests what is about to start.

Let's launch then into intractable metre (please
Note: accentual asclepiads), knowing your
Final term has begun ending – another spring
Too soon blown in a night-blizzard of pear-blossom.

In that garden you'd tend, under the Horse-shoe Hill,
Well you saw, with the straight eye of the countryman,
How soon after the rose aconites are in bloom.
So (since both of us loathe sentimentality)

What I'll wish for you won't be a perpetual
Leisured autumn, your decades of retirement come.
This mid-summer, you'll take armfuls of books back home;
Some you'll read yet again, shaded by apple-trees,

And maybe – out of old habit – you'll underscore
Well-loved passages you'd have us all learn by heart.
Then, from woods that stretch far off and away, you'll hear
Crow gold pheasants, a fox bark, sense elusive lines

Lift like otter-skin, sleek pelts in the glistening
Dark. Track them: for it's mint poems I'd want for you
All your weathers to come, season by season, and
Pure, rinsed light, as of this May-time, to write them by.

After the funeral

(for William Plomer, d. September 21st, 1973)

Home once more to a parched garden so sparse of flowers
It seems winter. The rose pergola bears one bud;
Here, good-humouredly, you chaffed my untidiness
Once, years back. It is hard, thinking of you as dead,

You now dumb. For the first time it is you not I
Who owe letters. I'll have, somehow, to do without
Your old-fashioned and unphonable presence who
Could be written to nights, mornings of blank despair

When no voice may be heard bearably answering back.
And, moreover, to whom now shall I send by post
Hard pears, Portuguese quinces and the home-made jams
You so savoured? Your heart stopped at the time of year

When fruit falls to the lawn harvested not by hand
But wind, cold, and a first frost that the tiring stem
Must yield to; when the great men in their severalty –
Casals, Auden, Neruda – would be taken, too.

Not young men: but their lives' work, unaccomplished quite,
Lies abandoned – a spade thrust in the earth, and left.
Now my garden's a lament for the makers. Small,
Red-brown, colour of blood days old, chrysanthemums

Turn tight buds to the sun. Tendrils of summer warmth
Clasp October; the leaves cling that you saw unfurl.
Not your elegy, this, William: it's much too soon.
Come year's ending, I'll mourn not for myself, but you.

Between acts

Worthing, the nineties; pier and promenade
Busy with bathchairs, wicker bassinets.
An upper window in the Esplanade
Releases smoke of scented cigarettes.

In this lacklustre town a masterpiece
Takes shape. Elsewhere, with all the earnestness
Of being unimportant, grim police
Take evidence. So does a mad marquess.

But play, as well as The Play, must go on.
In a hired boat, and 'rented' for the day,
The author dallies down to Littlehampton.

So, bathing in fame and briny on the way,
Hubristic yet, and yet to be reviled,
Sails Oscar Fingall O'Flahertie Wills Wilde.

Wild strawberries

They grew where no one
ever went but you
looking for something
else or for nothing
but some place beyond
places that you knew.

Sudden in fresh grass
you found them buried
alive in shadow
but ripening somehow
in the shade's stray warmth
where they chose to be.

At first they were few
as a baby has
little fingernails
and when you picked them
they lay on your palm
moments, finishing.

Sometimes there were more
but never enough
and year after year
you would come too soon
or late to find them
where they were before;

and those you tasted
ever afterwards
were only merest
evanescences

of those first berries
in a far-off wood

where your children go
in search of nothing
but what might be there
till the nights draw in
beyond the places
they know you know.

Gardener

New Year's Eve (a shag rug
the lawn, coarse with hoar-frost), rooks
spread wide wings in his emptied apple-trees.
They lift when he scares them

and caw, raucous, over the lily-pool.
Wafer ice is locking the apple-leaves
to tossed bundles, wads of dead feathers
after a rook-shoot.

All he'd wish this wintertide
is one more harvest, the barrowloads
he'd wheel back of another autumn's
superabundance.

Plots, look, are double-dug, pruning's done,
sleet blossoms into snow. Blunted light
in the creosote shed picks tools
lavished with Vaseline

tidy for spring. The floor stinks of fish-meal,
oil seeps from the power-mower. He longs
for the scent of clean, fresh-broken soil,
plunges a fist into

pressed moss peat that would burst from the bale.
Months must pass before next planting,
trowel and trug be draped with cobweb
and catalogues

keep from damp in orderly columns the seeds
he'll buy in due season. For the used earth
rests. Its limed clods will slide at the thaw
to crumble to tilth

in its own good time. Nothing, now, to tend
but bonfires. Today he crafts with tarred cord,
grease-bands. He smears, ties tight each bole,
while he remembers

windfalls, waspy, softening in the marigolds
where, also, the cricket ball fell
evening by evening till final summer collapsed
toward October.

His crops were ready, that first fall night.
Lifted potatoes in scattered patterns lay
through the dark to dry. In sacks he grappled them
muscular as wrestlers,

flung spent haulms to the yellowing pit.
Then: curds of cauliflower felt his knife,
ungloved were the fleshed broad beans, peas
rolled into colanders

and the kitchen busied. Kilner-jars stacked,
brim-packed with peaches and blackberries;
acrid in boiled vinegar, specked vegetables
browned into chutney;

red-currants, plums quobbled in the jam-kettle;
rhubarb and spinach bricked up the deep-freeze;
boxes crammed, ponderous the Conference pears
in tissue-paper.

And, as suddenly, the glut was done. Freed,
his pullets scratched and pecked all he'd missed.
The last Bramley picked, he replaced the ladder,
forked out the hen-house.

May cold sweeten the crudded litter, rain
leach it down. One more fortnight of surfeit
surely will come: enough to serve his own,
stuff to give away,

some that must waste or feed the wild birds.
He stares up, beyond his twigs, beyond his rooks
past space he is patient will brighten from solstice
into equinox.

Logs

Dumped from the truck, they
clobber onto themselves,
drum the outhouse walls
like yobs using boots.

Won't stack. I leave them
where they lie, my gnarls,
loppings, muddied chunks
and roots of a grubbed-up orchard.

Off-cuts, my father burns:
batten, deal, mahogany,
tongue-and-groove flooring.
From the way he warms himself

you can tell what a man is.
(Close, in a Tory park,
cord-wood dries for gentlemen;
stumps of elegant beeches

whiff like proffered snuff.)
To my hearth I carry smashed
kindling, crotched twigs.
Among the month-soft ashes

there are chars, knobby rusks.
Grudged, each flame I coax
from the load of rough fruitwood
tipped by today's gypsy;

any heat is won with skill,
stealth, furious bellows.
Late night, my fire shifts;
while I sleep, lyrically

flarings waste in an empty room.
I dread my craft, crabbed
words obdurate as sodden
bark: yet love the morning

scent of pear, the smoulder.
I might uncrumple a draft,
squatting at the grate the way
my father does. He holds

open hands to the bits
that catch, left of his labour.
I rake the slats of the fire-basket
for whatever embers, glad.

Perfidious Euterpe

I

Where does she keep? Assume her
among fusted arcana

in the mind's loft. The bitch
muse has hair liced as cottage-thatch.

Brittle as mouse-bone, her nails.
Her skin's the grey of dead gulls.

He remembers her pure white
before she learned to abort

with a filthy spike;
who sang with him once, awake

with child, feckful yet the sun,
and he not any kept man.

Nightly he gropes up
to her through the attic trap

of dreams. His mornings smell
like bleach on a hot blanched wall.

II

Four times a year she stirs him
to stare, glad, from a window
and say, *This is my season.*

March, it was an only snow
he glimpsed, like a pinch of moths;
In June, the scarlet beanflower

was nudged by bees; a pheasant
craked out of the first mauve hour
of Michaelmas; and an owl

creatured from December light
clung like a corbel under
his eaves. Always the glass clouds

over, though, from the sigh of
joy. When he rubs with his wrist
congealed and befouling breath

glairing the millimetres
between him and the insight
of fragments of happiness,

a left-behind glaze distorts
like oil on fresh rainwater.
Summer, spring, winter and fall

finish within the minute
of their beginning. The world
worsens, traduced with tears.

Rivers

Bridges are rare over still water.
Lagoons and lakes, offering
no grain to work against, we
circumambulate lengthily
but without rancour. Tactful
roads, visiting, soon leave
at arbitrary tangents. No –
like mountains, lakes and lagoons
don't seem to stand in our way:
containing within themselves
the weight of all their gallons,
they keep a place that is theirs.
Swiftly we cross in a skiff.
See how an expert oarsman
leaves prints on the waterskin
where piers would support the bridge
thrown by a megalomaniac.

Your river, though, is hostile.
Whereas brooks, rivulets
accept the simple homage
of two thick planks or a tree
felled or fallen, your river
makes insufferable demands.
Below where you may ford, vault,
leap or stepping-stone across
you must gawk at the far shore.
With what satisfaction one
would straddle the Amazon,
stooping to drink from its source!
Aping the caveman you can

swim, raft it over on logs ...
Hire mathematicians, else:
equations to do with bridges
are several inches long.

Beneath their arches congregate
all manner of disruptives
(lovers, derelicts, suicides,
the planters of gelignite)
while upright citizens cross
purposeful as salmon.
At nightfall, ruminative,
old men use parapets of bridges
to lean from and gob. Black
silkweed streams from cutwaters,
grips, is gone. Unfinishing,
rivers are always elsewhere.
Wade them after dark, cast
somewhere into their hissing,
feel how they clasp your thighs
as though they were the drowners.
See them slide under your shadow.

Barn owl

When it flies
it's as if
an owl shape
of chaff
had lifted off
floursacks

to sift
over straw
where shrews are
velvet shred
not far from
the barn-loft

where it will
unwinnow
afterwards
falling through
roof-ties and rafters
behind those eyes.

Zoo eagle

What with that quarried beak,
hewn hooks, eye
polished obsidian –
thou shalt not lift

such heaviness. But let
bone cantilever stress,
each wing girder stiff;
so, stiffen also

that chain-mail throat.
Grip tight to the dead tree
in the roof. Bear black
upon thy back. Be

that brass religious bird
of evensongs gone. Be
a struck gong. Plummet
once more. Rip into me.

Wild bird in a living-room

It means bad: starling
a slam and a slam
at the glass. We're shut
in a gadarene house,

our faces white from
a street accident.
We want it to die,
to shovel it out.

But it clutches books,
stabs the taut vellum
of a lampshade, drips
ticks from its soot feathers.

Its brittling legs
are a filth. Should we leave,
lie all afternoon
restless on a beach,

dried seaweed skirring
like flocks in the mind?
We stay, watching, grip
till light sucks it out,

fumble for the window-catch.
The room is exorcised.
Clean birds sparkle the grass.
We weep with sanity.

Fishing off the Isles of Shoals

I tear triple hooks out of mackerel
off land beyond land,

fling the spinner
bloodied back at the shoal, sense

(the cutter bucking through foam-water)
an aeon in the moment

of the surf-scavenging sea-bird,
when there crept

whatever gilled creature
tested the dry astonishment

of strand beyond tide
and found good to the touch

granules the long walking whales
(blunt fingers webbing over)

sluiced from unpuckered skin
before they swam with the tuna

scudding sheer across perennity where
I lave my hand in my wake.

Vipers,

sliding, pour themselves through themselves,
bits of miniature rivers.

Slack else, still
as worry beads left where they fell,

they abrade the young year's sun
in grit, green, brick, stucco brown,

a crumble. Always the eyes, coppery red –
sometimes the tongue, loose threads

flickering the wind.
This one I found

dead today, coils in a coil,
fills its Chinese bowl

with spent resilience. I'll keep it
as long as this takes to write.

Never before did I own a viper. Touch,
flinch,

to remember dry heaths of boyhood
summer, brackens, the sandy birchwood,

yelping in a pack for the hated snake –
deadlyadder. With a fork-ended stick

you'd fix his wriggling, knife his
sin. It was the lore of boys:

make a belt of the skin, heat
the flesh in an iron pan for the fat

that cures deafness.
Older, with a first girl in the sharp, dark grass,

you listened for the swift sibilance
of adders, appalled; and appalled in the silence

after, still you'd listen.
But, since, you've seen them often,

commonplace on an afternoon path,
exotic, arcane, tempting as death

to disturb. Several, zigzagged, ravelled as whips
lashed round themselves, whirls and loops,

finally subsided, a muddled tie-drawer.
One, disentangling, sloughed like a whore

peeling a stocking back. The new
head, mint as a pebble damped with dew,

had to be smashed. This one that's mine,
stiff in its small blood, its venom mine

for the simple milking, could kill
from posthumous spite. Did Adam, some residual

innocence left him in his great age,
lift the serpent's carcass in homage

to the nighthawk?
In the garden, to the dark

I commit this thing.
The fang

feels like red wire. I'd have
let this one live.

Mountain ponies

Driving before dawn, higher
than the kindling streams
where gradients were too steep
for grass, I glimpsed them,

life-like, a mirrorful
silvered on the dark,
gouged like a frieze
along edges of rock.

I stopped. They gazed
in sleep, nuggets
of fresh-hewn coal
their wide-open eyes;

still as an ambush;
necks thrust to the moon.
I disturbed no scree
of their freedom. Not

one coughed, not one shifted.
They thrived on hunger,
withers hawsered raw
by cold. I heard them breathe,

wished for them nothing
more than the grudged tack
of the mountain, the sunrise
that would hide them.

Creatures of a zodiac

I

The ram

is his testicles. Will serve
a hundred ewes, easy. Fat

wethers blether wifeless on
the long moors, delectable,

soft as shawls; but he, apart,
accepts his special food. Tough

in his sour wool he grows old
and uneatable. Will butt,

from machismo, anyone
with tender hands. In autumn

he sets about his labour;
looks over his Roman nose,

selects where to begin. Thumps
in ramstam till it's done, black

scrotum tight with tottery lambs.

II

The bull

Hard as a wall of sandbags,
he fathers herds in test-tubes.

A man in a clean white coat,
satisfied, washes his hands;

like udders, the rubber gloves.
At market, lot 22

got dumped from a Land Rover:
bull calf, born of a milk breed,

useless. It fell on its knees
like a Muslim at prayer. I

bid my sentimental pound.
In sharp suits, pie-men guffawed

and the auctioneer yawned
while I led Plug through kingcups

to a pond to drink the moon.

III

The twins

Am one person divided
by two. Might have made something

of ourself, but for this curse.
Did not ask for a lifetime

of needing no mirror. One
laughs because the other laughs;

likewise, weeps. One day one will
die. Until then, in the first

person plural, I and I
continue to amuse you

with our ambiguity.
Sometimes we, too, cannot tell

who is who. Forget about
twin love. Our identity

is hateful as a triplet.

IV

The crab

Catch him in the coldest sea
(the North Sea, the coast of Maine)

and keep him cold. Above all
keep him alive when you get home,

with seaweed in a bucket.
Call up your friend. At table

provide brown bread-and-butter
and *sauce vinaigrette*; a crisp

salad, well-chilled Muscadet.
Covertly, you'll have removed

the dead-man's-meat. Serve the rest
on a platter of crushed ice.

Eat. Regale your guest with tales
of crabbing at dawn. Do not

mention pans, the scalded eyes.

V

The lion

Inside the safari park
(Worcestershire, Great Britain)

we reach an *al fresco* vault
containing gold, the great cats.

The steel grill clangs as a white
hunter warns us: all windows

to be kept tight shut. We move,
tailgating tailgating cars

in a long, slow raft. We are
cooped in airless Africa.

Nostalgic for Birmingham
inhaling deep through its bricks,

I glimpse a bit of a tree
draped with a marigold rug.

Afterwards, we'll buy postcards.

VI

The virgin

still knows what we cannot know
ever again. O children,

before carnality, how
was the world? You are other,

discrepant not only for
your youth. Old nuns have skin as

unused but creased as linen
long-forgotten in a drawer;

they would smell of lavender
in the grave. Not religion

makes their special sanctity,
nor plain innocence yours. Flesh,

as soon as relevant, will
start to putrefy. We hold

holy what might have no end.

VII

The scales

An abomination, they
betoken parsimony.

God shall not be weighed. Sell me
stuff by the hunk, the armful.

Feed me in dollops. Exact
cooks lack the required panache:

great meals have no replica.
Avoid any man who deals

in micrograms, for he's up
to no good. Balance with hands.

As a rule of thumb, mice go
two to the ounce: lacking mice,

use judgment. A good judge will
toss in the guilty man's pan

a scrinch more of clemency.

VIII

The scorpion

Believe none of the legends.
If ringed with fire, it will not

sting itself to death. It will
die skittering with its fright,

flailing to the last, the way
humans do. Do not believe

it has no enemy. One
is dismembered in seconds

by army ants; with relish
it is gobbled down alive

by natives of Algeria.
Believe only (emptying

your shoes in Durango) that
Jove raised one to heaven: for

how else did Orion die?

IX

The archer

Sunday morning. A public
park, behind the tennis court.

Behold the bourgeoise figure
practising toxophily.

She is as old as England.
Fibre-glass flexes. She aims.

Her green person is bedecked
with thongs. Inside that leathery

head are fletchings, fistmeles, nocks.
Fifteen–forty on the court,

the server winds. A jackdaw
blows like a paper bag off

the cricket pavilion. Gold
equals Agincourt, Crécy.

Whizz. Thwock. Game, set and match.

X

The goat

Great-uncle kept a nanny
tethered to his damson tree.

She gave a gallon a day.
You'd drink some, warm, from a mug

made for the king's Jubilee.
We led her (when she'd be led)

by her chain to the churchyard.
Great-uncle was the sexton.

No sense taking a sickle,
he said, to grass that could spoil

in the summer rain. And so
we drank from grandfather's grave

and from *his* father's father's.
The milk was sweet. Sour damsons

fell when she butted the trunk.

XI

The water-carrier

I am required and always
shall be while men move ever

from springs of purest water.
Beyond where there are flowers

they glance up at my coming.
Though they are glad to see me,

let no one think I am loved.
They grudge the small pence I ask.

I am working against God
Who intended waterless

places. No one pays for spilth.
My shoulders are forever

raw from the rub of the yoke.
Shall I be damned? It is worth

more than souls to slake deserts.

XII

The fish

Is it limblessness makes them
alien? Sometimes they will touch,

with bellies deft as chiffon,
some swimmer come to their midst.

They move, lissom, from nowhere
to nowhere. For them there is

no unnecessary death;
they do not get left to bleed.

They are unaspiring, like
all finished things. God's perfect

artifacts, they need evolve
no more. (Though, could they grip with

more than their mouths, what cities
might rise from the sea?) They do

not know they cannot be mad.